The
Aquarius Personality

Understanding Your Own
Innate Aquarius
Personality Traits and
Characteristics to Become
a Better Aquarius Woman

by Laney Thomlin

Table of Contents

Introduction

Have you ever been told that you are highly independent and strong-willed? Or maybe you feel that's true about yourself without having anyone else say so. But these two characteristics only begin to scratch the surface of who you are as an Aquarius woman. It's time to get to know the rest of the inherent Aquarius personality traits that may be buried deep within you, so that you can learn how to enhance them and use them to your advantage!

If you go through life not being aware of your intrinsic astrological personality, you might not be able to explore your full potential — which is essential to becoming a better version of yourself and ultimately succeeding in life. Not only is it important to nurture and develop your strong suit, but it's equally as important to correct (or compensate for) the negative characteristics as well. As you learn how to overcome these negative traits, you can readily triumph over the adversities in life.

This book is designed to help you better understand yourself as an Aquarius woman, and to thereby assist your growth and personal fulfillment. So if you're ready to learn more about yourself from the inside out, then let's get started!

Chapter 1: The Innate Personality Traits of an Aquarius Woman

An Aquarius woman has her own personality traits that are worth cultivating and optimizing for their best use. Aquarius individuals (those born from January 21 to February 19) have Saturn and Uranus as their ruling planet. The Aquarius basic element is air; that's why your lucky color is purple or sky blue. Your lucky days are Wednesday, Saturday and Sunday, and your lucky numbers are 1 and 7. Your birthstone is amethyst, and your symbol is a water carrier. As an Aquarian, you have the following positive traits.

Innate positive personality traits of an Aquarius woman

1. Freedom loving

Aquarius women are innately independent. They love their freedom and would rather be out in the world, than stay tied to their chairs inside the four walls of their offices. They hate being told what to do because they want to be free to do what they want. They do, however, enjoy advising other people on what to do.

2. Impartial

They are impartial in approaching issues, so they can be superb judges, evaluators and critics. In this aspect, they are similar to Librans, who view both sides first before rendering judgment.

3. Good listener/great conversationalist

Those born under the Aquarius sign are good listeners and hence, are also great conversationalists. They can listen patiently and wait for their turn to speak. They allow other people to express themselves fully.

4. Dynamic speaker

Aside from being able to listen well, Aquarians can also speak fluently. They are dynamic speakers, who can charm a crowd and capture their rapt attention with their words.

5. Loyal

The Aquarius woman can be expected to stick by their partners and commitments. They stay loyal whether as a friend or as a business or life partner. They take a long time to commit, but once they do commit, they stay loyal and faithful.

6. Adventurous

They love adventure and exploration. Aquarians would actively seek to go on new adventures rather than stay cooped up at home.

7. Intelligent

They are intelligent and willingly search for new knowledge. They have a profound desire to learn and enrich their knowledge.

8. Rational

They use their brain foremost before anything else. They won't choose to act based on their emotions. They have to think a hundred times before embarking on any activity.

9. Ingenious

They can think out of the box and create something out of nothing. Their imagination is immense and fervid with new ideas and thoughts of things they can invent and create.

10. Sociable

The ever amiable Aquarius loves company, and basks in other people's attention. She is the life of parties, and has no trouble befriending anyone and everyone. Her wit, charm and pleasing personality can attract both genders.

11. Pleasing personality

Aquarian women are easy to like and love because they have a pleasing personality. They know how to put their best foot forward and how to be on the good side of each person they meet.

12. Extrovert

Together with their sociability is their extrovert trait. They prefer going out and partying or being amidst people and having fun.

13. Leadership skills

They possess natural leadership skills that make them the obvious choice to lead groups because of their outgoing personality.

14. Visionary

They are forward thinkers who can envision incredible things that should and need to be done and attained. These are the people who invent new things to solve current problems.

15. Generous

They love to give to the needy and the disadvantaged. They enjoy doing social work and similar activities.

16. Truth seekers

They aspire to seek the truth whenever possible. They don't want lies or half-truths. You can trust that they will only speak and want the truth—no more, no less.

Innate negative personality traits of an Aquarius woman

No one is perfect. Just like everyone, Aquarius women have less than desirable characteristics and traits. The following are the traits you can improve on:

1. Unemotional or cold

Because of the Aquarian's innate nature to stay rational, people often misinterpret this as being unemotional, cold or detached.

2. Stubborn

A corollary to their loyalty, they stick to their own decisions, once they've made them. But they don't decide rashly, they think it over carefully, so their decisions are usually smart decisions. They tend to be stubborn and follow their own mind. This can be a problem when they are working with other people because decisions should be made as a consensus of the majority.

3. Rebellious

Due to their stubbornness, they can become rebellious. Aquarians are known to cause a disruption in an organization when they violate rules or protocol due to stubbornness.

4. Sarcastic

At times, they can also be sarcastic without meaning to. It's just in their nature. They have the tendency to say something mockingly that gets under other people's skin, but they have no intention of hurting anyone.

5. Habit to procrastinate

Aquarius women tend to procrastinate due to their social nature. They would rather go partying and postpone what they are supposed to do at the moment. This can be a problem when deadlines have to be met.

These are the innate positive and negative traits that Aquarians generally possess. Understandably, you will possess these traits to varying degrees; certain ones you won't manifest at all, while you may indeed identify characteristics in yourself that are not even listed here.

Chapter 2: How to Enhance Your Aquarian Positive Traits

Now that you know your innate positive traits, the next step is to maximize this knowledge to become a better woman and live your life to the fullest. How can you do this? Here are the essential guidelines:

1. Your love of independence

If this trait is still buried deep inside you, you have to allow it to become evident in your personality. You can cultivate it by spearheading freedom movements in your community, such as gender equality and similar causes that you feel strongly about. You can also establish your independence by living apart from your parents, or earning your own money.

Make decisions on your own, or if you are married, let your partner understand that he has to respect your independence in certain aspects of your married life. You have the freedom to choose your own clothes and your own friends. Other examples are:

- Freedom to pursue your own career goals

- Freedom to choose whether to have sex or not

- Freedom to stay safe and healthy

You can maximize this trait starting now. Consciously believe that you owe it to yourself to enjoy this freedom.

2. **Your impartial nature**

You can easily develop this trait by practicing it every day. Remember that it's already in you, so it takes a little unraveling to reveal it. Visualize removing the skin of an onion to reveal its inner portion. Here are activities that you can engage in to hone this trait:

- Volunteer as a judge in contests

- Act as a mediator between two conflicting parties

18

- Decide between two choices

How to develop impartiality:

➢ Know both sides of the coin. Research all available angles about issues, parties or personalities concerned.

➢ Rely on proven facts and clear evidence; not on hearsay or circumstantial evidence.

➢ Judge the merit of all available choices, based on all facts involved.

➢ In cases, where there are two parties involved, the solution must be recommended and approved by both parties. Allow a freewheeling discussion between both groups. Then they should compromise and come up with their own solutions.

➢ Guide them to select the best choice, after careful deliberation.

➢ Ask yourself the question: "Can the choice be beneficial to both parties or to all parties concerned?" If your answer is yes, then it's the best choice.

3. Becoming a good listener/great conversationalist

You can be a good listener and a great conversationalist by observing these tips.

- When another person is speaking, don't interrupt.

- Listen attentively by showing your interest to the speaker through your actions. You can nod your head, smile, or look him straight in the eye.

- When it's your turn, speak clearly and in a well-modulated voice.

- Ask about the other person's interest, and don't speak only about yourself. Remember that other people are not usually interested in your educational qualifications, honors received or status in life. Mention them only when asked for this information. Keep in mind that most people are only interested in themselves. Observe how a person's eyes light up when you ask him about his family or his achievements.

- Enrich your vocabulary daily, so you can carry intelligent conversations.

- Read, read and read. Make a habit of reading the daily newspaper for your fill of current events around the world. Read up on various topics so you can contribute significantly regardless of the topics that come up during conversations.

- Don't monopolize conversations. You're not the only person gifted with intelligence. Give others the chance to speak their mind.

- Be considerate of the other person. Don't talk about topics that are taboo to him.

All these tips can turn you into a great conversationalist. Strive to observe them every time you converse, and you'll soon find out that people love to spend time chatting with you.

4. Becoming a more dynamic speaker

There are no inborn fluent speakers. Even the outstanding Greek orator, Demosthenes, started as a bad speaker. Whether or not he really trained by placing pebbles in his mouth, what we do know is that he practiced continuously, even to the extent of orating in the open sea. Becoming a dynamic speaker is not easy. Even if it's already innate in you, you still have to cultivate it. Here are steps for you to follow to hone your speaking skills.

➢ Believe in yourself. You can never become an excellent speaker, if you don't believe you can do it. This is the first crucial step.

➢ Acquire the habit of reading. Reading will broaden your knowledge and allow you to speak confidently about various topics.

➢ Prepare a short speech and practice speaking before a mirror.

➢ Practice public speaking by asking questions during a meeting. You can also volunteer to speak about certain topics, or conduct a short lecture on important issues. Start with a small group, and then shift to bigger groups.

➢ If you have stage fright, learn how to conquer it, by constant exposure. Don't give in to your fear. Deal with it head-on by exposing yourself repeatedly to audiences until you get used to it. You can perform deep breathing exercises before the speech to help you relax and forget your anxiety.

You have to constantly practice until you sufficiently develop the skill. This is an innate trait that you should uncover because it can propel you to success in all your undertakings.

5. Loyalty

Yes, you're a loyal and faithful partner. Use these traits wisely. Pledge your loyalty and fidelity to people who deserve them. That's why you have to be judicious in choosing your partner and your friends. To show that you are loyal and faithful, let the following pointers guide you:

- Defend friends and associates when other people speak ill of them

- Stand up for them in times of crises

- Be there when they need you

- Show your love and concern

- Stick faithfully to your partner no matter what. Don't play with fire. You'll get badly burned in the process if you do. It's a stigma you don't want to undergo. Being

24

faithful will bring you peace and love.

6. Sense of adventure

Develop this trait by welcoming adventure into your life. Explore all that the world has to offer. Go camping with friends. Travel around the world. Explore the tourists' spots in your area with new eyes. Life itself is one big adventure, so live your life to the fullest by being open to new adventures and opportunities.

7. Intelligence

You're intelligent by nature, so don't wallow in the doldrums of your imagined dumbness. If you still haven't maximized this trait, then start doing so with these simple steps:

➢ Train yourself to think intelligently by believing in your own intellectual capability.

➢ Practice replying promptly and accurately when a question is asked.

➢ Continue educating yourself about your own profession. Enroll in continuing professional education courses to learn more about your field of expertise. Knowing more about your own field will enhance your intellect.

➢ If you're a student, there's no substitute to becoming knowledgeable than reading and studying. Study your lessons well and you'll excel. Avoid cramming, but study daily instead, and you'll reap the rewards of scholarship at the end of the semester.

➢ Whenever you open your mouth, say something substantial and don't spew nonsense. People will know whether you're dumb or intelligent through the words that you speak. Hence, say sensible and intelligent things only. To be able to do this, you must be knowledgeable. To be knowledgeable, you have to keep studying and learning.

8. Thinking rationally

This is a good trait when dealing with problems. Emotions often get the better of people, causing them to make rash decisions that can ruin their lives forever. You can develop your innate ability to think rationally by constantly practicing self-control and the following behavior:

- Keep calm when making decisions.

- Don't use your emotions to decide. If you are emotional, allow some minutes to pass before acting or passing judgment.

- Remind yourself to act judiciously as opposed to acting rashly.

9. Creativity

Your ingenuity can be cultivated by your conscious engagement in creative ventures. The creative juices are there, but you have to use them so your mind will get used to their availability. Here are activities that can enhance your creativity:

- Sit down and write. Don't bother about syntax and grammar. Just write down your thoughts as they come. Let your ideas flow freely and record them. You can edit later on, after the deluge of thoughts cease to flow. When you do this daily, you can develop your writing skills. Later on, you can read books about writing and grammar to enrich your writing prowess.

- Get a blank canvas and a set of paints and create your own world with a brush. Don't think about painting the best picture. Just paint whatever you want to paint. Let your creativity shine through. Express yourself on the blank canvas. Skills are developed through time, so keep at it.

- Invent new things that can be beneficial to you and to other people. Aquarians are inventors. Think of new items or ideas that you can introduce. It doesn't matter how small it is, as long as it's useful. It can be a matchbox container or a spoon chest. The paper clip is a small invention but it made the inventor, Johan Vaaler, a millionaire and a self-fulfilled person. You can be like that too, if you believe in your own ingenuity.

- Take up a musical instrument and create wonderful music. Let your spirit soar with the notes and sounds of songs. Again—don't think that you don't know anything about music scores and the like. Just tinker with piano keys or guitar chords freely; the rest will eventually fall into place.

- Solve problems the creative way. Yes, you can practice creativity by solving problems. Thinking out of the box when coming up with a solution is creativity. There are several ways to skin a cat, so don't limit yourself to the common methods. Think like a child and let your imagination roam. An example is the following puzzle:

Connect all the dots inside the box shown below without lifting your pen.

Here's one solution:

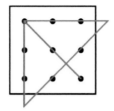

If you try to solve the problem by thinking "normally", you won't be able to. The solution actually requires you to think out of the box; notice how the lines went beyond of the boundaries of the box in order to solve the problem.

Here's another solution:

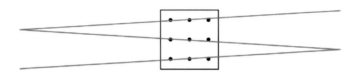

You now know what I mean. Let your imagination flow freely and you will be enhancing your creativity. This is a valuable innate trait that once developed, will take you to new heights in your endeavors, in your career and personal life.

10. Being sociable

The ability to relate to others well is one trait that every person wants to acquire. Many people are shy and, as much as they want to socialize, they lack the ability. In your case, you have it in you. You can enhance this trait by doing the following:

- Go around and interact with friends at gatherings.

- Introduce yourself to new people. You have that innate quality to be witty, so don't hesitate to unleash your charm. Apply the pointers on being a good conversationalist that were presented earlier in this book.

- Approach a new classmate and talk to him.

- Welcome a new neighbor.

11. Cultivating a pleasing personality

You are naturally pleasant to everyone. You don't like hurting other people's feelings. But, in case you are still not aware that you have this in you, here are activities you can do to bring out this superb trait.

Smile. It's the greatest make-up you can wear on your face. It's also easier to smile than to frown. You would be surprised at how it can transform a gloomy face into a beautiful, happy face. People love people who are happy. A smile can also be infectious. It can pass from you to another person, and that person can pass it on to another.

- Respect other people. Don't look down on anyone. Think of people as equals—not objects to be used or abused. Be kind to everyone, because the people you meet on your way up may be the same people you will meet on your way down. Love begets love, just as respect begets respect.

You want other people to respect you, so give respect as well. Respect their privacy by not invading their private space, not reading their mails, not gossiping about their lives, not backbiting them. Speak respectfully to them. The many ways you can show your respect towards others are almost always easy to do.

- Be kind. The way you treat people, who can do nothing for you, reflects your own character. Help the old lady cross the street. Share an umbrella with a stranger during a rainy day. Give shelter to a stray cat. Of course, use your common sense too, because there are bad people out there, who may take advantage of your kindness.

- Develop your sense of humor. People love to be around a person who can brighten up a tense atmosphere. Learn to find humor in stressful situations, and enjoy a good laugh when needed most.

12. Leadership skills

You're a leader, and you simply have to claim it. You may need a little buffing to bring out your "shine". Here are activities that can do that quickly:

- Volunteer to be the leader of a group assignment.

- Act as the speaker of an organization seeking justice.

- Volunteer to spearhead an office event.

- Act as the proponent of a new policy in your institution.

There are thousands of ways to become a leader. But take note that a leader is someone who is not bossy (orders people around), but someone who "leads" through example. If you want to be a good leader, be a good team member first.

13. Developing a vision

This trait is related to your ingenuity trait. Visionaries are typically people who can create new opportunities that can be beneficial to everyone. You are an entrepreneur who can create novel ways to solve problems or institute dynamic changes in your environment. You can also practice the activities recommended for the cultivation of the traits ingenuity and independence.

14. Generosity

Develop this trait by actively participating in social work, such as donating to charitable institutions and doing social work in jails or in homes for the aged. You can also donate to your local community's development projects.

15. Seeking the truth

You always pursue the truth in things that matter to you most. If you haven't known this in yourself yet, it's time you do. Hone this trait by doing the following:

- Always tell the truth, unless it's a matter of life and death. An example is when a Nazi is pursuing someone you know and you have to lie to save the person's life. But, aside from this type of situations, always tell the truth.

  As they say, one lie always leads to more lies. This is because you have to lie continually to cover up the previous lie. In addition, it will go against your innate trait and your conscience will bug you no end because this is not "you".

- Encourage others to be honest as well. As the song goes, "Honesty is such a lonely word..." But it doesn't have to be that way. Visualize a world where everyone lies. It is a chaotic place that you don't want to live in.

These steps recommended here are only a few of the things you can do to enhance your Aquarian traits. Be open to learning and seeking more ways to develop and grow to become a better individual.

Chapter 3: How to Get Rid of the Negative Traits

Your bad traits are your stepping stones to becoming a better person. Turn your lemon into lemonades by converting these unwanted traits to positive ones. More importantly, you will find that the conversion process will strengthen your character.

1. Excessive emotional detachment

You don't have to become unemotional or cold to be rational. Being rational doesn't mean turning off your emotions. It simply denotes keeping your emotions at bay. Here are activities that can turn your coldness around:

- Empathize with a friend who has lost a loved one. Put yourself in her shoes and imagine how you'd feel. Or maybe, empathize with a friend who has lost a cell phone. Visualize yourself losing your phone, and imagine how it would feel. Then express your empathy

41

to her. Show some genuine
emotion.

- Be one with a friend whether she's
  happy or sad. Express it with both
  words and actions. Remember that
  you're innately a good person, so
  you must dig in deep within
  yourself to counter this negative
  trait.

- Before a mirror, practice showing
  your emotions with facial
  expressions and gestures. When
  you show emotions, make sure
  they are genuine.

With constant application, you will gradually
shed off your cold and unemotional façade.

2. Stubbornness

Being stubborn can become a negative trait, if
you don't want to give in even when you're
wrong. You can miss incredible opportunities
if you don't get rid of this negative trait. Don't

let this happen to you. Listed below are
activities you can do to eliminate this trait.

- Learn to accept when you're
  wrong. Being stubborn about an
  idea you favor, even when you
  know you're wrong is being dumb.

- When there are activities that you
  have planned and someone
  suggests a better idea, welcome
  the idea. It can hurt your ego a
  little bit, but a confident person
  like you with a good self-image
  can live with that. No one single
  person has all the best ideas, after
  all.

- If it's not truly significant to you,
  give in to small requests that come
  your way.

3. Your rebellious nature

While innate, your rebellious side stems from
your independent and freedom-loving nature.

Try consciously practicing these actions to curb your rebellious nature:

- Learn to say "Yes". Don't disagree with every idea presented to you. There will be good ideas that will deserve your affirmative reply.

- Abide by the rules of the group you belong to. Rules are there to maintain order. Whenever you notice yourself about to violate a rule, consciously remind yourself that it's a negative attitude that must be eradicated. Unless the rule is flagrantly violating people's rights, you have to follow them.

- Understand that your rebelliousness stems from your love for freedom, so follow your love for freedom and independence, but learn not to overdo it.

4. Sarcasm

Being sarcastic is the negative aspect of your trait as a dynamic speaker. Because you can express yourself fluently, sometimes you tend to be sarcastic. The following tips can help remedy this:

- Be cautious of what you say by being mindful of what might hurt others.

- Say what you want to say properly. Don't say something while smirking or pouting; it can be misconstrued as being sarcastic.

- Make it a habit of being truthful in a good way. Eschew sarcastic remarks because they can be mean and hurtful. You can say: "You look gorgeous, let me just fix this ribbon…" instead of saying sarcastically: "Wow, you're dressed to the nines! Look at that ribbon." There are things that you can say in public and those that you can say in private. A little amount of respect will help you decide which is which.

5. Procrastination

Procrastination is not good. It can prevent success in your goals in life. Here are recommended activities that can help you eliminate this negative trait:

- Don't give in to the urge of postponing what you're supposed to do for the day. Practice this habit daily, and be persistent in doing it until you can easily disregard procrastination.

- Finish one task in one sitting. Don't stop unless you're done, especially if it's a short task. Acquire this habit and you can successfully conquer this unwanted trait.

These activities can help you overcome negative traits. You cannot get rid of these habits quickly, but it is not impossible. Be patient, consistent and persistent and you will emerge victorious.

Chapter 4: How to Become a Better Aquarius Woman

Conscientiously working to become a better woman will turn you into a better person, one who is equipped with the traits to triumph over the adversities of life. It's a noble goal that's worth all your valiant efforts; hence, be persistent and keep on keeping on. To lead you in your pursuit, here are simple steps you can use as your guide.

Step #1—Enhance your positive traits

Take note of your positive traits and start enhancing them. If they're still not apparent in your personality, perform the recommended activities in Chapter 2. You have to do them consciously every day until they are inculcated in your subconscious mind and become second nature.

Step #2—Get rid of your negative traits

Be aware of your less pleasant traits and decide firmly to get rid of them for good. With an optimistic behavior, you can do it. Don't stop until you have effectively eradicated them from your system. It takes a Herculean effort to do it, but you can as long as you persist. No one can ever be perfect, so expect this to be among your lifetime challenges. Should you fail, keep standing up and restart your efforts to eliminate them all over again.

Step #3—Love yourself

Your aspiration to become a better woman will be a lifetime process. You cannot achieve this easily. It will be a constant struggle. The mere fact that you're willing to undergo the challenge is a noble feat in itself. Therefore, learn to appreciate yourself—the total "YOU". No matter who and what you are, you must learn to love yourself. If you don't love yourself, who else will?

Step #4—Learn how to appreciate other people

As you learn to love yourself, learn to appreciate the people around you too. This will make you aware of whatever actions you commit. Are your actions not inflicting injury to the people around you? If you appreciate people around you, you'll always think of their welfare. You become a better person, only when people around you become better because of you.

Step #5—Keep going and live life to the fullest

Don't be discouraged by failures. You have to keep going and live your life to the fullest. You only live once, so make the most out of it.

You can never predict what life has in store for you, but by being positive, you can choose to enjoy life, be happy and have fun.

Chapter 5: Ten Tips for Personal Growth

You, as an Aquarian, will encounter people whose Zodiac signs will conflict or be harmonious with your own. Knowing how to deal with them can signify triumph on your part. Being able to capitalize on your positive characteristics and being able to conquer the negative ones is a noteworthy accomplishment. To help you manage the challenging task of relating effectively with others and of conquering yourself, here are tips to guide you.

1. **The Aquarius woman is compatible with Gemini, Libra and Sagittarius men.** You have some common traits with Sagittarius, such as love for adventure and vibrancy. You and Libra are both sociable beings, so you'll both enjoy interacting with people. Like the Gemini male, you love fun, adventure and social interaction. You'll enjoy spending time exploring the world with these gentlemen.

2. **As an Aquarius woman, you're incompatible with Scorpio, Pisces and Virgo.** Most Scorpio men are possessive and are introverts, which contrasts with your outgoing and independent nature, so better be

ready for a clash of personalities. On the other hand, Pisces men are needy and demand quite a lot of attention, while Virgo men are usually nitpickers, who are skeptical of new ideas. These traits will slowly mar your independent and freedom-loving nature and will cast a cloud of doubt in your relationship.

3. **You are highly likely to succeed professionally as an inventor, teacher, entrepreneur, politician, actress, writer, and musician.** You can succeed in careers that need ingenuity, leadership and social skills. You're a smart, amiable and great person, so you can flourish in any career you set your heart to.

4. **Your erogenous zones are your ankles and your calves.** You may want to explore this fact with your sexual partner.

5. **Your partner must be imaginative to be able to satisfy you in your sexual relationship.** Keep in mind your need for exploration and adventure in choosing a partner in life. Although of course, sex is not everything when choosing a partner, sex can play a huge factor in a couple's compatibility.

6. **Learn to be constantly aware of your actions.** A greater personal awareness will aid you in correcting your negative traits before you commit blunders.

7. **Share your knowledge with other people.** You're an intelligent woman, and sharing what you know will help other people, while allowing you to etch that knowledge even deeper in your memory. Sharing information makes it valuable because more people benefit.

8. **You're prone to illnesses related to the bones, heart, bladder and central nervous system.** Hence, take extra care of all related organs.

9. **Your independent, rational and ingenious traits will help you triumph in any business venture.** You have the characteristics of a good business leader.

10. **Engaging in social work will help make your life complete.** Because of your kind and generous nature, and your love for people, an active participation in society will bring you self-fulfillment.

Conclusion

Your innate Aquarius personality traits are your aces for overcoming your problems and becoming a better woman. As you continue to grow and improve on your personality, you will be amazed as you become more aware of the various beautiful facets of the unique person that you are.

Be brave to apply what you have learned from this book, and don't be stymied by pessimistic people. You create your own life by the choices that you make. Choose to maximize your innate characteristics and emerge a winner.

Finally, I'd like to thank you for purchasing this book! If you enjoyed it or found it helpful, I'd greatly appreciate it if you'd take a moment to leave a review on Amazon. Thank you!

Made in the USA
Middletown, DE
02 November 2018